EVERYTHING
SUMMED UP

Overcoming differences and loving
your neighbor as yourself.

RACHEL LOVINGOOD

Cover Design: Mackenzie Waters

Text Design: Mackenzie Waters

ISBN-13: 978-0-692-16327-6

Published by Impact Resources, Tennessee

EVERYTHING
SUMMED UP

RACHEL LOVINGOOD

RACHEL LOVINGOOD

To Trish,

Who could have known (other than God) what would happen when we moved in across the street from each other on Windham Circle?? Those years are ones I cherish and reflect on often. Thank you for allowing me into your life and sharing your thoughts with me honestly.

You are one of God's great blessings to me and I love ya sister!!

P.s. Jeff still thinks his yard looks better than yours...

RACHEL LOVINGOOD

For the **commandments** "You shall not commit adultery, You shall not murder, You shall not steal, You shall not covet," and any other commandment, are **summed up** in this **word**: "You shall love your neighbor as yourself."

—— Romans 13:9 ——

TABLE OF CONTENTS

Introduction

I have a confession.

I'm kind of a cut to the chase type of person. I like the summary sentence that tells me the most important facts and I've even been known to say quite often, "okay, here's the deal," in order to help a discussion along. This is not something that I bring up much or ever brag about BUT then I realized that I'm not the only one that likes a summary recap.

In Romans we can find one of the best sum it up statements ever! Check it out in 13:9 "The commandments, "You shall not commit adultery," "You shall not murder," "You shall not steal," "You shall not covet," and whatever other command there may be, are summed up in this one command: "Love your neighbor as yourself. (NIV)"

How awesome is this? I love it because it packs so much truth into just one verse and takes off a lot of pressure we could feel from trying to remember and keep up with many commandments. It all gets taken care of if we just learn to love our neighbors as ourselves.

Simple.

But not always easy. Right? At least it hasn't always been easy for me over the years (I'm not necessarily blaming my neighbors but...) just kidding. The truth is, some of my neighbors throughout the years have been super easy to love and some have been downright tough.

1

But there is no distinction to only love the neighbors that are easy to love. We are called to love our neighbors. Period. Even if they are nothing like us-and let's be honest, those are usually the toughest ones to love.

That's the premise of this study. How can we do a better job of following this one simple commandment that sums up all of the others? This is a subject that is very close to my heart because God has taught me so much through this process. My motivation comes from a real life neighbor experience that wrecked my world and changed me forever (thankfully).

I had a neighbor that was the complete opposite of me. Annnddd we definitely did not get along or have much in common. Yet God had placed us both there for a reason so I kept trying and she was new to the South, looking for friends so she was ok with me trying to connect with her.

God taught me so much through our friendship. Much of it was because she was brutally honest about what she thought and what she had been taught as she grew up basically removed from the church.

Through our conversations and interactions I learned about what so many people (me included) need to know when building relationships with people who are different from us. Whether those differences are cultural, racial, generational, socio economic, ethnic or anything else—they are not necessarily easy to overcome unless we are intentional about some things.

That's what you will find in this study. None of the things you read will be earth shatteringly new to you BUT hopefully will help you make some changes that God can use to reach people for the sake of the Gospel. So let's talk about:

HOW TO USE THIS STUDY

Confession number 2:

I don't always remember things. Now this might be an age thing or just a fast paced world where we all multi task a lot thing but it's a real issue. I HATE to mess up and miss something important and I bet you do too.

The other day I was headed out to do several things and an alert popped up on my phone reminding me of a scheduled event. That one little reminder changed the course of the rest of my day and I was SO SO grateful it did! Whether you tell Alexa to remind you about something, set an alert on your phone or write things on sticky notes to post where you can see them, we all can benefit from reminders.

That's what this study has:

Reminders.

Things to challenge the way we are going about our days and help steer us in a different direction in developing relationships for the sake of the Gospel. That's a big deal and although nothing you find here will probably be all that new of a thought—each of your "Reminders" will be things that can help you be more intentional as you live life and interact with people that God has placed in your path.

You can walk through this book however it best fits your life. There are 6 Reminders with study notes, thoughts and application. Feel free to do this on your own or if you choose to study as a group there is a group discussion guide in the back for your meeting times.

However you plan to use it just please USE it. Don't let this be another study that you add to your stack of finished books BUT let it transform your life and your relationships as you apply what you are learning or at least being 'reminded' of. There are people who need Jesus all around us—when are we going get serious about reaching them 1 at a time??

If you're wondering why it matters think about this:
You + lost person can = eternity when they see how real your faith is and they want it for themselves.

1 + 1 = eternal life in heaven
That's worth it.

So whether you add the things you're studying as notifications on your phone or put them around you in sticky notes or write them on your hand in marker—do something to keep these relationship building tools in front of you to challenge and remind you.

Praying for you and for God to use you!!!

EVERYTHING SUMMED UP

Reminder One

RELATIONSHIPS ARE THE KEY

A majority of people are won to faith in Christ through relationships. What role did relationships play in your own salvation experience?

List the names of people who had an influence on your faith:

When you think about those who were part of helping you see your need for Christ, it may remind you how very important it is for you to become that kind of person. Do you care enough about the lost and unchurched to develop relationships with them so they can find Jesus? Mark where you fall on this scale:

Do anything so that
others can come to Christ

No time to put into
others problems

Many of us will say that we care because we know that is the right answer but when you look at your life do you see evidence that you're living like you think it's important?

I remember a time when I was at a student crusade prep rally (my husband was the student pastor) and we were challenged to think of 5 people who didn't know Jesus that we could commit to pray for and then bring them to the crusade. I just sat there completely convicted that I had no lost friends. I was very involved at church and doing things that were good things but I had surrounded myself with church people and had not been intentional about getting to know any lost people. Honestly, I've always been pretty good at justifying my behavior but there was nothing I could say to the Lord as He began to speak to me.

It hit me that in being busy serving the Lord and leading in ministry I had forgotten one of the most important things we are all called to do—"Love my neighbor as myself". If I really love people then I should want them to know Jesus, I should care about their souls enough that I'm willing to get to know them and let them see Jesus in me so that hopefully they will come to want a faith like mine.

Are those people that God has put into my sphere of influence, who need to know Him, worth the time and energy it takes to be friends?

Yes   or   No?

And that's where it starts to get sticky. Too many of us who call ourselves Christians are so busy doing that we don't have time to be Jesus to the lost and unchurched. Instead of thinking about finding extra time to devote to these relationships, think about who you already come in contact with, in the schedule you already have, that may be someone who needs Jesus. Use this graphic to identify people who are already in your life that you can just become more intentional with about Jesus.

7

- Write your name in the middle
- Label the spokes with the places you go regularly (school, church, neighborhood, work, ball park, Sonic)
- Then draw lines off of each spoke and list the people you encounter regularly at each place, that you don't know are Christians
- You may not even know their name, so list them by description
- See page 60 for a larger version to tear out and keep with you

Excellent!! Now that you see there are people around you, let's talk about how you can be more intentional about actually developing relationships with them. It will take being intentional because sometimes this is one of those things that is easier said than done...

NO ONE WANTS TO BE YOUR PROJECT

Describe the difference between treating someone like a friend and treating someone like a project.

Do you understand why this matters? No one wants to be considered valuable only for how you can change them. I don't blame them because neither do I. What are some ways that we treat people like projects? Check out the list below and add any you can think of.

- Only spending time with them in order to ask them to something else that has to do with my faith.

- Spending all my time around them talking about my faith and not getting to know them.

- Making my interactions with them all about my schedule and focusing on them when I have an agenda.

-

-

-

-

-

-

These are just a few examples. I'm sure you can think of others but the common factor to focus on is that treating people like a project is more about me and what I want from you than building a relationship because you're a valuable person.

What does Romans 5:8 remind us about the lost people around us?

Exactly! We are all sinners and every person on earth is someone that Jesus died for. That makes them beyond valuable as a person!!! If we truly want to reach them with the Gospel then we need to get to know them as a person.

GET TO KNOW THEM SO YOU KNOW HOW TO INVITE THEM

The majority of lost people will not jump at the chance to go to church with you. They may shy away from going to a small group or Bible Study---UNLESS you know them well enough to know how to invite them.

Consider this. When you invest in a friendship with someone then you will become familiar with what draws them. Do they like large crowds and loud music? Small groups and deep discussion? Sports and competition? There are all kinds of Christian activities in your life that you can bring lost people to if you know which ones interest them most.

I was trying to get a lost friend to give Christians a chance. Her previous experiences had not been positive; I knew she likes game and is super competitive so I asked her to come to a game night that a group at church was doing. She loved it and was blown away by "how nice all those Christians were" and that "no one looked at her funny for being there".

Sometimes all it takes is knowing what will interest them enough to introduce them to other believers and more doors get opened.

Think about some of the lost people in your life. Write down their names and what you know about them that can help you know how to invite them in order to give Christians a chance and hopefully reach them with the Gospel.

NAME	CHARACTERISTICS

KNOW WHAT THEY'RE THINKING

This is not that easy unless you either remember being a lost person or you have an honest friend who does. What happens is that we get so used to being around Christians that we have no clue what lost people are thinking. I was so shocked to realize that my lost friend who moved in across the street thought it was awful that she had moved in near me---her words about living with ministry wives on two sides were "I thought I had moved to hell"---and that is not due to anything other than me being a Christian.

Get this. Lost people are NOT impressed with Christians in general. Their perceptions are strongly influenced by Christians they see in the media and ones they have had negative experiences with in the past. *How have you seen this to be true in your interactions with the lost and unchurched?*

Some other common thoughts of the lost and unchurched we need to be aware of are:

"You think you're better than me."
—Why do you think this is a thought lost people deal with in relation to believers?

Probably because we are always trying to get them to change and choose Jesus. (We still want them to choose Jesus but need to temper our approach so that we don't come across as thinking we are better than anyone else.) What can you do to help change this perception?

Freely admitting that my life is not perfect. I'm not perfect, and things don't always go my way is one of the best ways I have overcome this. We are all imperfect sinners in need of grace. Make sure they know you feel that way.

"You're judging me and my choices."
–No one wants to feel judged by someone else. It makes us defensive.

How have you ever felt judged? How do you react?

What ways do you sometimes make people feel judged?

It's important that we speak truth in love like the Bible tells us to but knowing when to speak is key. You don't have to comment on everything and when you do make sure that you don't sound arrogant or judgmental.

"You think you have all the answers" —Now this is challenging because Jesus really is the answer but it's tough to get close to someone who always knows the answers. We need to keep this in mind and sometimes do more listening than talking.

These are just a few common thoughts that people who aren't familiar with believers tend to have. You may think it isn't fair for them to lump us all together but we as Christians do the same with non believers…. until we get to know them. That's why we need to be intentional about relationships so we can all get to know each other for who we really are.

I was shocked when I began to understand some of the typical thoughts that my new friend had about Christians.

Yet I am often guilty of some misguided thinking myself—like, *"she doesn't want to talk about Jesus or spiritual things because if she did she would ask me"*. NO WAY—they are as intimidated by you as you are by them. When we buy into this wrong thinking then we fall into roadblocks to relationships.

WARNING: Don't Assume

I remember assuming things about my lost friend like, *"she's heard this before and just doesn't care, or "since she's an atheist she must have chosen to reject Jesus."*

BUT I couldn't have been more wrong. She told me that she had heard of Jesus, and had even seen Him on the cross on a wall but she had never heard the gospel. She had no idea why Jesus was on the cross, or that He didn't stay there but died for her sins and rose again on the third day.

Although I couldn't believe that someone could grow up in this country and never have heard the Gospel message-it hit me that I was guilty of assuming things that weren't true, and I failed her in so many ways because of that.

What happens if we continue to assume things like this about lost people?

Why do you think it's valuable to know how non-believers think?

What are some things you will do differently to better understand how they think?

Who have you been guilty of assuming things about that may have led you to miss opportunities to share with them?

How have you seen assumptions lead to prejudices?

What is the danger of prejudices in developing relationships?

People really are watching to see if your lifestyle lines up with what you say you believe. How you live your life matters—a lot.

How have you seen this to be true both positively and negatively?

How do you feel when you hear someone talk about their faith then see them live differently?

Use this journal page to write out prayers for people you're trying to reach and to keep notes on what you're learning about them and yourself.

If you really keep the royal law found in Scripture, "Love your neighbor as yourself," you are doing right.
James 2:8

Reminder Two
CHARACTER COUNTS

We live in a world that quickly rejects that which looks irrelevant or fake. Including Christians who say one thing and then live very differently. If we have a real faith then our lives should reflect that—in every area.

What are some areas of your life where your words or actions don't always line up with your faith?

- ○ Language
- ○ Social media
- ○ Marriage/family
- ○ Gossip
- ○ Negativity

- ○ Dating relationships
- ○ Work/school
- ○ Fun/entertainment
- ○ ....
- ○ ....

Most of us have heard the saying "talk is cheap". Another saying that applies is this one " I can't hear what you're saying because what you're doing is speaking so loudly." Hmmmm good word-right? How many times have you ignored what you heard someone say because you were so distracted by how they were acting?

17

Why do you think actions speak louder than words so often?

Especially in this day and time, words seem to come much more cheaply than ever before. When you put your words into action it takes more effort and this speaks strongly about what you really believe and what kind of character you actually have.

One of the most common excuses lost people use to stay away from church and things of the Lord is that church has too many hypocrites. We will never be perfect at dispelling this attitude but it is smart of us to keep it in mind as we reach out to invite people to know Jesus.

How can keeping this thought in mind affect your decision making?

One way to consider this whole character counts concept is to consider advertising. Have you ever been influenced by some ad on TV or elsewhere then when you actually got the product it didn't live up to the advertisement you had seen? You got taken in by false advertising. It's the bane of any good shopper and it fits in this discussion today.

You and I as believers in Jesus Christ are His advertisements to the lost world. We need to live our lives in such a way as to make people want what we have. That means that the posts we put on social media, the expressions on our faces in the slow line at the store, the way we treat servers in restaurants and all the other ways we influence and interact with the public, matters a great deal because we are either drawing people toward Jesus or sending them the other direction.

I love what I used to hear in student ministry. *"If you are the only Bible someone reads what will your life say about God?"* That's kind of scary that we really can be the only Bible or Gospel that some people will ever see and yet it is true. Sad to say but so often we treat our responsibility cavalierly and carelessly—that's our sin.

Check this out. When you make even small godly choices it can teach others truths about who God is.

Match up the actions with the Truth about God from Scripture that shows what people can learn from watching us.

WHEN I	THEY LEARN
Giving food to a homeless person	Forgiveness is real and possible
Inviting neighbors over for coffee	Someone cares about me
Not holding a grudge	We need each other
Returning extra money when you receive too much change	I'm a person of value—no favorites to God
Helping an elderly person with yard work	Integrity is still alive
Giving up your seat to another in a crowd	My needs matter

Honestly, no choices are too little to matter. God told us to be careful about how we live. Look up Gal 5:15-16 and answer the questions.

What are the two choices of how we live?

Which would you rather be?

Why do we need to be careful how we live?

It would be hard to argue against the fact that we live in evil days if you pay attention at all to the happenings around us. It stands to reason that if the days are evil then we need to be more careful than ever how we live our lives.

How would you describe why it matters whether you make wise or unwise choices in these evil days?

Here is another summary statement to help you:
Live it or you have no hope of leading it and sharing it with others.

My friend said it this way, *"Be sure that what you are slinging around is something that will attract people NOT turn them away."*

What do you need to do differently in light of this reminder that your character counts?

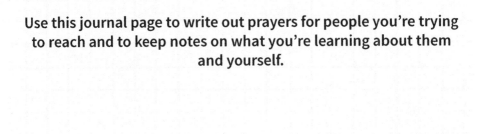

Use this journal page to write out prayers for people you're trying to reach and to keep notes on what you're learning about them and yourself.

Love the Lord your God with all your heart and with all your soul and with all your mind and with all your strength.' The second is this: 'Love your neighbor as yourself. There is no commandment greater than these.
Mark 12:30-31

Reminder Three
BE AUTHENTIC

We live in a world that spins things, filters things, adjusts things, and posts only the highlights to the point that it becomes difficult to know what is real. Social media has only increased the temptation to wear masks and pretend like we have it **all** together **all** the time.

I hadn't really thought about this much in terms of my faith or my witness. Then my friend shared her testimony in church after becoming a believer and when they asked her *what did Rachel say that made you know you needed Jesus?* — I had a HUGE wake up moment. I was all set to write down what words of wisdom I had shared in the course of many conversations that were those most powerful words that led her to Christ.

Then she answered the question and I will NEVER forget what I heard. She said, "It wasn't anything she said. It was when she let me in her house when it Was dirty, when her car wouldn't start, when I knew she was mad at her husband and when I saw the biggest pile of dirty clothes I have ever seen, that I realized she had a real life with real issues and a real faith and then I started to want that."

Wow! Did you get that? Although it is very important that we talk to people about Jesus, what we also need to remember is that being authentic is vital because authenticity leads to evangelism and evangelism is what we are here for.

It's a mistake for us to think that we need to live our lives pretending to be something we aren't in order to impress the lost world. What actually has more impact is for us to live *real* lives with our *real* faults and issues and let them see our real faith. THAT is what makes the difference and it is very freeing to us as believers.

Unfortunately this is also an issue with the church. **Why do you think those of us in the church struggle with authenticity?**

....

....

Right. There are a lot of things that push us to put on a mask or pretend that things are more perfect than they really are.

One of the ones I have had to work through is the feeling that if people know what I'm really like then they won't like me or respect me any more. Which is the biggest for you?

Be sure to consider the influence that social media has on our quest to be authentic. We spend a HUGE amount of time looking at posts and pictures from people that often feed our own insecurities. This is so dangerous because it feeds a competitive feel that can create distance between us and our 'neighbors'. It also builds a sense of discontentment with what we have, how our house appears, how our kids act, how we look and just about everything else!!

How have you seen the habit of comparing your real life to everyone else's highlight reel affect how content or discontent you are?

Read Philippians 4:11-13. What can you learn from Paul about being content?

According to verse 13 what is available to help you be content?

If you are wondering what being content has to do with building relationships with lost people, consider this. Feeling jealous or competitive with someone is not conducive to developing friendships and living authentically.

Annnddddd neither is the other end of the authentic spectrum—TMI. You've probably noticed that some people like to air all their dirty laundry and tell everything on social media or in person and then call that being 'authentic'. The problem with this is no one needs to know all that about you. One key to living a Gospel centered, authentic life is finding the balance between hiding behind a mask and too much information.

Which do you lean toward more: Hiding behind a mask or telling too much information?

We've already thought through why authenticity matters why do you think telling too much information can be detrimental to building relationships?

If you tend to tell *too* much *too* often to *too* many people you may need to check out Psalm 62:8.

Who does this verse tell us to 'pour out our hearts to'?

Yep. God. He alone can handle all of our everything and when we make it a habit to go to God first then it's amazing how that changes our need to talk to someone else or post about something that happened or 'vent just a minute'. He gives us perspective and insight that tempers our need to spill our guts to others.

What good can happen when you pour out your heart to God first?

This is a discipline that can help with every aspect of your life and all your relationships. Go to God first and let your life be a witness and testimony of how you aren't perfect but you serve a God who is and is all powerful.

Too many church people think we win the lost by beating them over the head with our morality and shaming or guilting them into the Kingdom. That only pushes them away farther.

In actuality we will change people's minds through the life transforming power of the Gospel that must be evidenced in our own life change! **Live it in order to share it…**

What do you need to change in order to live a more authentic life?

Use this journal page to write out prayers for people you're trying to reach and to keep notes on what you're learning about them and yourself.

You, my brothers and sisters, were called to be free. But do not use your freedom to indulge the flesh; rather, serve one another humbly in love. For the entire law is fulfilled in keeping this one command: "Love your neighbor as yourself."
Galatians 5:13-14

WATCH YOUR WORDS
Reminder Four

What you say is a big deal. As you get to know people who need Jesus-they keep a close watch and ear on what you say—whether it is **verbal** or **electronic** communication.

Proverbs 18:21 tells us about the power of the tongue. **What are the two things mentioned?**

Death and Life. Two complete opposites and yet your words can carry the power of each. Impressive and intimidating. Words can do so much good and so much destruction.

Read the following verses and note what else you learn about the tongue or words we use.

- James 1:26
- James 3:5
- 1 Peter 3:10

29

AVOID "YOU SHOULD"

One thing that is tempting (but dangerous) for us to do as our unchurched friends become more interested in spiritual things is to load them down with all kinds of **'you shoulds'.**

As they lean more towards things of faith, an easy approach for us to take is to fill their heads with *"you should get in a Bible Study"*, *"you should get a Bible"*, *"you should join the choir"*, *"you should get involved in a group"* and so on. You get the point.

Yes. Those are all good things, but to a brand new person in church circles, that's a lot to take in. My friend actually brought it up to me by asking if I wanted to know what almost made her turn away from her new direction towards Jesus. My response? Um, yes of course I do!!

That's when she told me about the 'you shoulds' that pressured her and made her feel overwhelmed. Overloading new or young believers can actually have the opposite effect—it can make them retreat from things of the Lord, or just give up because they feel they will never measure up.

This doesn't mean that we don't care about their spiritual growth, but it means we don't just dump a list on them. Doing life together is what it's all about. As you walk through life with each other, you speak Truth into their lives. They ask questions and you both follow the Holy Spirit as He leads in growth.

At some point you can also find a Bible study or discipleship material to go through. The key is not to force them into things but to share with them through your own learning experiences. One thing I realized was that my goal is not to make my friend into a clone of me but to help steer her to grow through God's Word into who He has created her to be. There's a big difference.

She always reminded me that she had a completely different background growing up than me and that she still had years worth of tapes that played in her head to overcome one by one with the Truth. I liked to remind her that God has good plans to use her with her unique background and circumstances in ways He couldn't use Maybe we all need to remember this truth.

Who are some people that you know God brought across your path that needed your uniqueness?

How have you seen or experienced overloading people with "you should" having a negative effect?

NO CHRISTIANESE

Another aspect of watching our words ties to using Christian language that makes others think they need an interpreter.

Think about how some of our regular 'christian' terminology could be confusing to the unchurched:

- **Die to self**
- **Listen to God**
- **That was ordained**
- **Pray about that**

Any of those phrases that seem so natural to us after time in the Word and in church, can sound like a foreign language to newcomers. My friend said she was so confused all the time at first and wondered when the preacher said "Paul said..." if he was talking about Paul McCartney or who. She told me, "I felt like such an outsider and that I wasn't part of the club when I didn't understand so much being said. I just wanted to find Genesis in the Bible!!"

Why do you think it's detrimental for newcomers to feel like outsiders when Christians talk in our own lingo?

If our faith seems like a club that excludes certain people then we are not being as effective in reaching the lost as we are called to be.

Some other statements that create more confusion or feelings of not belonging in newcomers are things like:

- **"I know you've all heard this before..."**
- **"As you know in the story of _____..."**
- **"Of course you know all about _____..."**

What if you had never heard a verse of Scripture before and when you sat down in a church service the speaker started out with one of the previous statements? Would you feel welcome or not? Would you want to stay or ever come back?

We need to remember many people that we come in contact with (yes even in America) have not had the privilege of growing up in church or in the Word of God for many different reasons. Our calling is to share Truth with them in a way that offers them the opportunity to come as they are and feel like God's Word is for them too—even if it is brand new to them.

One day after hearing a sermon that really rocked her world and made her start to question a lot of things about faith, I tried to explain to my friend what she was confused about. I was quoting John 3:16 and using it to validate the Gospel message she struggled with. I actually used the words "you know like in John 3:16…" She looked me straight in the eyes and said "No, you still don't get it. Every time the preacher reads a verse of Scripture out loud, it's the FIRST time I've ever heard that verse in my life."

I was stunned. She was 30ish years old, grew up in the United States and had never heard any verses of Scripture? That was so crazy to me and it hit me like a ton of bricks that I was way too clueless about the unchurched. Tears came pouring down my face and I will never be the same from that moment on. It was such a powerful lesson to me and a great moment for our relationship as friends and sisters in Christ.

What are some other common things we might say or hear in church circles that can make new people feel left out or like they don't belong?

Star any that you've been guilty of saying and commit now to being more careful about your 'language'.

Look at what Paul (the apostle) wrote in 1 Corinthians 9:20-23 about this issue. What is the ultimate goal? What is he willing to do to reach people with the Gospel?

That is the same attitude we need to have. Are we willing to set aside our own comfortable groups and lingos in order to invite other into our lives and share Jesus with them so that they might know Him as their Lord and Savior?

Would you say that you are right there with Paul, willing to sacrifice and do things differently than is most comfortable for you if it means people coming to know the Lord? Where would you fall on this scale?

I refuse to change   I'll do anything

What are the things that hold you back the most from being like Paul? Mark any that apply or add your own thoughts.

- Fear
- Comfortable the way I am
- Apathy
- Never thought about it
- If what I say isn't clear that's their problem
- Other_____

Once we realize where we tend to fall short we need to do something about it. **How can you be more intentional about the way you talk that will make lost people more receptive to the Gospel or at least building a relationship with you?**

Before we leave this topic consider this—sometimes even when we are being clear about what we say it can have the opposite effect. This was sort of mentioned earlier when we talked about what lost people think about Christians but think about it a little more.

More than one new believer has told me about this and it's pretty valuable to know. When Christians say some things that is NOT always what is heard by a lost person:

When we say "I'll pray for you" that can actually be offensive to someone who doesn't know Jesus because it can communicate "you think you're better than me". It can also be interpreted that we as Christians think something is wrong with who we are talking to or that think we have all the answers. Although we know prayer is good and helpful, they don't, and so sometimes when we say that we are praying for them it comes across as arrogance.

One friend told me that she used to cringe when someone said they would pray for her, and get mad because she didn't want anyone telling God where she was or what she was doing. She said, "I didn't want to be pointed out to God because, to me, He was a mean angry judge who was waiting to smash me like a bug."

Here's another common phrase that usually isn't received well by lost people: "That's part of God's plan". When they hear that in relation to something difficult going on in their lives then they think, "Wow, if that's part of God's plan then He really has it out for me, and must really not like me at all." It reinforces their negative and faulty perception of who God is.

How does it make you feel to realize how inaccurately skewed some people's perspective is of God?

....

....

Who do you know with a faulty perspective of God? What can you do to help them overcome that and see Truth?

....

....

You may be thinking, *"but I want to pray for them and for them to know the power of prayer"*. You can. One of the most powerful things we can do for others is to pray for them, but instead of forcing it or assuming that they will like it. Ask them.

Just say "Would it be ok if I pray for you about that?" It makes a world of difference and takes away much of the resistance. Although I have had people tell me no before, it's more common that they agree. And even if they tell me no, I can still pray. I just don't have to broadcast that I'm praying until they are ready to receive it.

Use this journal page to write out prayers for people you're trying to reach and to keep notes on what you're learning about them and yourself.

'Do not seek revenge or bear a grudge against anyone among your people, but love your neighbor as yourself. I am the LORD.
Lev 19:18

Reminder Five
LET THE HOLY SPIRIT BE THE HOLY SPIRIT

It's exciting to choose Jesus! Do you remember what it is like to wake up and realize that you are a new creation in Christ? That your old self has died and you have a whole new life through Jesus? That you have forgiveness for your sins and you now receive grace and mercy on a regular basis?? That's good stuff and unfortunately many who have walked with Jesus for a while have become a little more ho hum about these things.

One of my favorite things about walking through life with new believers is their passion and how it stirs my own passion in so many ways. May we never get lackidaisical about passion for Jesus and do everything in our power to continue stirring up that passion in everyone around us.

That's something to discuss and stay intentional about. Some of our churches are not only not *seeker* friendly, many are also not very *new believer* friendly.

One thing a lot of new believers want to do is get involved but in many churches there is a 'club' mentality that tends to limit what new people are allowed to do. There is typically a group of people who are the ones who have led Bible Studies and groups for years without any need for newcomers. This type of mentality limits the reach of our groups and also limits the potential growth of our people.

Often we send new believers off to serve in the nursery and that may be the giftedness of some, but consider that others who are new to the faith may have the gift of leading or even teaching. **Our job is to nurture that in them and offer opportunities for them to grow as the unique Christ follower they are.**

How can always using the same leaders over and over lead to a type of spiritual rut or limit growth of all the people?

....

....

This doesn't mean that leaders need to be put away after a certain time but look at the value in bringing new folks into the leadership circle by pairing up a seasoned leader with a newer Christian.

What are some benefits that can come from pairing a seasoned believer and a new believer in leadership roles?

....

....

What are some places you serve where you could invite a newer believer to come alongside you?

....

....

This is a fantastic form of mentoring and discipling that works wonderfully. I love seeing how the passion of new believers can fire others up as they inspire and encourage people to believe that God really does make a difference in **everyday life** and eternity!

One of the keys is letting the Holy Spirit be the Holy Spirit. Yes, if you're like me then you may have some practice at being the Holy Spirit. BUT that is not the best plan. This kind of goes back to not overwhelming people with all that they "**should be**" doing, but is actually a little more proactive.

We need to remember that the Holy Spirit is the one who saves and draws people to Christ—He just allows us to be part of the process sometimes.

Write out Philippians 1:6:

Who is the one who began the good work?

And who is going to complete the good work?

In light of that, it's vital to remind ourselves that the Holy Spirit is the one who will direct the growth and transformation of each believer. We still have a role to play but the Holy Spirit is the only one who can do His job.

One of the most important roles we play is one of encourager or coach, and here are a few things we can practice to make us more effective.

SCRIPTURE HAS THE ANSWERS

When people ask me questions I always try to steer them back to scripture for the answer. It's vital to model a reliance on Scripture to those that are new to the faith. It also never hurts to remind any of us that God's Word is the absolute Truth and none of us have all the answers. We can also use those questions to demonstrate how to look things up in Scripture and how to search for answers to our questions.

What are some other benefits you can see to sending people to Scripture for the answers they need? What are the negatives if we just tell them our opinion?

....

....

You may have thought of the value of teaching someone to rely on scripture instead of on a person, or that the sooner a person 'owns' their faith the stronger it becomes. We want to always let God use us but never get in the way of what He wants to do in someone else's life.

DON'T OVERREACT

This one can be hard for some because we are so passionate about various things and issues. BUT it is also crucial because when we miss this and overreact then we hinder future communication, sometimes to the point that they stop asking us questions.

Picture this---what if your new believer friend (who has a very different background and maybe different political affiliation) comes to you with questions about something like:

- **Abortion**
- **Alcohol drinking**
- **Drug use**
- **Immigration**
- **Racial issues**
- **Sex outside of marriage**
- **Homosexual relationships**
- **Politics**

And you freak out. Overreact and get a little crazed trying to make a point you firmly believe in. **What could be some possible consequences?**

That doesn't mean that we shouldn't care about tough, controversial issues and even take stands for ones we believe in, BUT we also want to recognize that everyone, especially a new believer, may not be at the same place as us on any given subject.

My friend grew up totally opposite from me. In. Every. Way. As she grew in faith, the Holy Spirit brought things up in her life that she had to wrestle through with Him. We also had another very passionate, political, mutual friend who would get very dogmatic about subjects like the ones just listed. My new believer friend would not go to this other person with questions because her passionate answers felt more like an aggressive attack.

How can you relate?

43

What are some issues that you've had to wrestle through with God until you came to an understanding?

What would've been different for you if you asked questions on the subject and been blown away by someone's aggressive, passionate response?

Over reactions can stunt their growth, quench the Spirit or steal their joy—all of which we want to avoid.Be aware that even though a person comes to Christ he or she will not automatically become a cookie cutter Christian who thinks the same as us on every topic and frankly that shouldn't be our goal.

Read 1 Corinthians 2:16---who are we all supposed to be thinking like and becoming like?

....

....

Exactly. Jesus. And becoming like Him or developing a mind like His happens through the work of the Holy Spirit. So give Him the freedom to do what only He can do in your life and everyone else's too.

Do you trust that He will convict and challenge as necessary—on His time table, not necessarily what and when you think growth should happen?

....

....

It's a control issue. We need to be reminded again and again that we are NOT in control. God is and He will work according to His perfect timeline...

Did you get that? Timing is everything.

No matter how much you want change and transformation to happen, God's timing is the key.

Think about some of the "perfect timing" moments you've experienced with the Lord. I love being able to look back at some incredible moments in my life and see that, even if I didn't recognize it at that moment, God was working all things together for His purposes. AND I love that He will continue to do that if we just let Him be in control and trust His timing.

What do you need to do differently to let go of control and trust In God's timing?

Use this journal page to write out prayers for people you're trying to reach and to keep notes on what you're learning about them and yourself.

Jesus replied: "'Love the Lord your God with all your heart and with all your soul and with all your mind.' This is the first and greatest commandment.
And the second is like it: 'Love your neighbor as yourself.' All the Law and the Prophets hang on these two commandments."
Matthew 22:37-40

Reminder Six
ENJOY THE RIDE

This last reminder is probably the most fun for me. As I have had the privilege to walk through life with some fresh new believers, it has been one of my most favorite things to do. I LOVE experiencing the life of faith with those who are new to it.

Whether it's the casual way they bring up some deep theological issue to discuss—like the time I received a text that said "Explain predestination.."

What?!?! In a text??

Or that time when my friend stopped by my house in a furious mood and plopped her Bible on my counter while saying, "I won't be needing that anymore."

Realizing that something big must have happened I asked, "Really, why not?" Which set her off on a tirade along the lines of "Did you know that Moses doesn't get to go into the Promised Land??" (completely indignant)

47

After schooling my face, I said "Well, yes, I did know that." And she went off into how that "burned her up because Moses has busted his butt for those Israelites, took care of them, and put up with all their whining and complaining. Then just because of a little mistake, he doesn't get to go into the Promised Land!!!"

In that moment she didn't need me to lecture her on why that was the reality or explain anything. She just needed me to listen and let her work through the Scriptures on her own. I didn't need to go on and on about why she shouldn't quit reading the Bible. I just let her walk back out of my house when she was finished, and I trusted that the Holy Spirit who was wooing her would draw her back into the Word as only He can. So I just rolled on the floor laughing and enjoying every minute of her righteous indignation for poor old Moses.

Just a couple hours later I heard my back door open, saw a hand reach around the corner to pick her Bible up and without a word head back home.

What are some of your favorite things about doing life with new or young believers?

We need to remember these things, celebrate them, and thank God for them because they continually remind us to look outside our circles to see who else needs Jesus that we are bumping into in our everyday lives.

I hope these reminders of very simple things that we can be intentional about have helped you as much as they changed me. It's not rocket science I know but sometimes the simple things can get lost in the busyness and we need to be reminded to make them a part of our lives. It's actually all just principles and practices we can see in Scripture.

There's one story found in Acts 8 that illustrates what each of these tips and reminders looks like in practice. Let's finish up this study by walking through the story of Philip and the Ethiopian eunuch for a recap of all 6 reminders in action.

Read Acts 8:26-28

Now an angel of the Lord said to Philip, "Rise and go toward the south to the road that goes down from Jerusalem to Gaza." This is a desert place.
And he rose and went. And there was an Ethiopian, a eunuch, a court official of Candace, queen of the Ethiopians, who was in charge of all her treasure. He had come to Jerusalem to worship and was returning, seated in his chariot, and he was reading the prophet Isaiah.

Who directed Philip where to go?

When we are living in the Will of God then He is placing us in strategic places to encounter people He intends for us to impact with the Gospel.

Who are some people in your life that could need the Gospel?

49

Get this. The Eunuch was reading Scriptures and had been worshipping. But unless Philip was paying attention to the Lord and those around him he wouldn't know this.

v. 29-30

And the Spirit said to Philip, "Go over and join this chariot."
So Philip ran to him and heard him reading Isaiah the prophet and asked, ("Do you understand what you are reading?")

What could Philip have made assumptions about in this situation?

He could have assumed that since the man was part of the royal crowd that he wouldn't be interested in things of faith, or that since he was reading aloud Isaiah that he was already a believer.

Notice the power of asking questions. Instead of jumping to conclusions or making assumptions, Philip just asked an innocent yet pointed question. Do you understand what you're reading? Pay attention. Ask questions.

v. 31-33

And he said, "How can I, unless someone guides me?" And he invited Philip to come up and sit with him.
Now the passage of the Scripture that he was reading was this:
"Like a sheep he was led to the slaughter
and like a lamb before its shearer is silent,
so he opens not his mouth.
In his humiliation justice was denied him.
Who can describe his generation?
For his life is taken away from the earth."

What was the result of Philip's question?

Yes! It opened the door to further conversation and connected the two men. Also by asking the question Philip didn't come across as a spiritual know it all or an arrogant person who thinks he has all the answers. He just showed that he was interested and cared about the situation. It revealed that God was at work.

What are some signs that God may be at work in some others' lives that you are in contact with?

Sometimes it can be that they are starting conversations about spiritual things, it can be that they are frustrated with their life or circumstances, it can be that they are running out of hope or that they are questioning their existence or purpose.

We don't have to know all the answers or the whys we just need to be observant and ready like Philip was.

v. 34-35
> And the eunuch said to Philip, "About whom, I ask you, does the prophet say this, about himself or about someone else?"
> Then Philip opened his mouth, and beginning with this Scripture he told him the good news about Jesus.

Check it out! One simple question, an open door and God does great things.

Where did Philip go for answers when the eunuch asked questions?

Back to Scripture. Many of us are scared to start Gospel conversations because we are afraid that we may not have the right answers when someone asks the hard questions. (and believe me they will ask!) But that's perfectly alright because Scripture does have the answers and we can direct people straight to God's Word. Also remember that no one likes a know it all so it is actually beneficial to say, "I'm not sure about that, but we can look it up."

What are the other positives of responding with, "I'm not sure about that but we can look it up."?

v. 36-38

And as they were going along the road they came to some water, and the eunuch said, "See, here is water! What prevents me from being baptized?"
And he commanded the chariot to stop, and they both went down into the water, Philip and the eunuch, and he baptized him.

Can you sense the excitement in the Ethiopian man? He finally had some answers to his questions and a brand new sense of purpose.

Philip just responded to the Lord's perfect timing and helped with the next steps. He didn't load him down with a bunch of "you should" he just let the Lord lead.

v. 39

> *And when they came up out of the water, the Spirit of the Lord carried Philip away, and the eunuch saw him no more, and went on his way rejoicing.*

This part of the story is hardest for me because it reminds us that God brings people into our lives in His timing and sometimes it is just for a season. I absolutely LOVED the time I spent across the street from my neighbor for so many years.

In that time our story was very different from this one in Acts 8. I had the opportunity to have my passion for Christ stirred by her faith. To enjoy seeing the Word come alive to her for the first time. To have the challenge to stay in the Word myself so I could keep up!

This was especially true when she decided to read through the Bible for the first time and started a blog for accountability. She had over 300 people join her on her quest to read thru the Bible in a year. It was quite the adventure!!)

Our own spiritual journey don't stop, but rather as we invite newer believers along on our journey it pushes us and raises the bar for both of us. It's a win win. I wouldn't trade the lessons I learned, the fun we had and the God moments that changed me, but then we moved. God called us to another place, a different church and that's good. Hard but good.

I get the privilege of watching her powerful transformation continue to be used in mighty ways through social media and long distance. And I rejoice. I am forever grateful and will take all I learned and keep going forward for the sake of the Gospel building new relationships and being intentional.

Who has been there for you for a season?

What impact did that relationship have on you?

Have you ever thanked them or let them know how your life is different? *If not, then consider doing that now.*

It is my prayer that these simple reminders will motivate you to be intentional about relationships with lost and unchurched people. Do what you have to in order to make them part of your every day life because we are all living, working and doing life around people who are nothing like us.

It is time for us to stop, listen, ask questions and invite them into our lives and our faith. For the sake of the Gospel. Because as Jesus said, "everything is summed up with this 'love your neighbor as yourself".

It really is that simple.
Everything's summed up.

Use this journal page to write out prayers for people you're trying to reach and to keep notes on what you're learning about them and yourself.

"You are the light of the world. A town built on a hill cannot be hidden. Neither do people light a lamp and put it under a bowl. Instead they put it on its stand, and it gives light to everyone in the house. In the same way, let your light shine before others, that they may see your good deeds and glorify your Father in heaven."
Matthew 5:14-16

GROUP
DISCUSSION GUIDE

Introduction

- Take a few minutes to get to know each other by sharing your name, something about you and why you chose to do this study.
- Lead a discussion of why this topic matters—why we should be people who reach out and share our faith with the lost and unchurched.
- Go over the Introduction in the book together Pages 1-4
- Share a personal story about how some kind of "reminder" helped you recently.
- Make a list of all the different kinds of reminders that people use today.
- Lead a time for each person to share what kind of reminder they use most often and why that works best for them.
- Ask: Why do you think "reminders" may be helpful for us in our spiritual lives and especially in sharing our faith?
- Share that prayer will be a valuable tool for your group times and decide what kind of ongoing prayer list you will keep as a group so that you can all be praying for each other and for the people you want to reach.
- Types of list suggestions:
- Posterboard
- Electronic form—such as google doc or email list or group me list
- White board if you have a permanent meeting place
- Other_____

Discuss any questions anyone has about how to do the study or meeting times or snack options.

Close with a prayer time. You can choose to do prayer partners or pray as a group but spend some time asking the Lord to give you courage and boldness as you walk through this study. Remind the group that they should expect spiritual attacks as they strive to become more intentional about living out the great commandments.

Reminder One
RELATIONSHIPS ARE THE KEY

- Start by displaying a key ring or a bunch of different keys. Show how there are many different kinds of keys but they still achieve the same purpose of opening doors. Point out that the "reminders" in this study are just common phrases that most of us are already familiar with and the first one is about relationships.
- Lead members to share how relationships affected their own journey to faith in Christ.
- Point out the story on page 7. Ask: When you read that Rachel couldn't think of 5 lost people to be praying for, what was your reaction? Why?
- When you completed the graphic on page 7, were you surprised at how many lost people you are already coming in contact with? Why or why not?
- Point out that the same graphic is on an appendix page on the back of the book so that you can reproduce it and then tear it out of your book to post or carry with you as your prayer list.
- Discuss the difference between treating people like a project and building a relationship.
- Go over the list on page 8 add to it as a group.
- Lead a discussion of how getting to know people will make it easier to invite them. Be specific and share any insights from your chart.
- Ask: Were you surprised to read that lost people are not impressed with Christians in general? Why or why not? What is our responsibility in light of this revelation?
- Refer to page 11 and discuss responses to the questions about being judged.
- Encourage each person to share what stood out to them the most from Reminder 1.
- Close in prayer and add names to your collective prayer list as you share any updates about conversations each person is having with lost and unchurched people in their spheres of influence.

Challenge members to share honestly so that you encourage one another when fear strikes, or a conversations doesn't go well or the response is not ideal. Remind others that obedience to do what God is calling you to do is a win, even if it doesn't go perfectly and when an opportunity is missed then share that and pray for another opportunity to arise

Reminder Two
CHARACTER COUNTS

- Share an example of a time when you were a victim of false advertising. It may be something you ordered from an infomercial or bought off the street in New York. Make the point that false advertising is frustrating for the buyer because "what you see is not necessarily what you get."
- Relate that concept to the reminder for today by asking people to share (without naming names) an instance where they experienced a person's actions or words not lining up with their claimed faith. How did that make you feel? Why?
- Ask: How guilty are each of us at this also?
- Point out the list on page 14, allow each person to share which area of their life doesn't line up with their faith the most.
- Share responses to the question "why do you think actions speak louder than words?"
- How do you respond to the criticism that church is full of hypocrites? (remind people that we are all hypocrites at some point and so of course churches have them since we are all sinners in need of grace but at least we are actively striving to overcome that sin.)
- Discuss the matching exercise on page 16 and as a group share some other examples of what people can learn about God from our actions.
- Read Galatians 5:15-16 aloud. Ask; What did God say to you from these verses and the questions on page 16.
- Discuss responses to the last question on page 17.
- Share personal requests about the people each member is sharing with and add any names to your collective list. Encourage each member to share what God has taught you about your character and pray for each person in the group to be wise about their decisions this week and to make the most of every opportunity.

Reminder Three

BE AUTHENTIC

- Display a couple of items that show the difference between real and fake. (plants, fruit, etc) Use whatever to get the conversation started about the value of being real or authentic.
- Why is authenticity an issue in today's culture?
- What are some of the challenges against us being authentic?
- Share responses to the question of why authenticity is a struggle on page 19.
- What is your own greatest personal challenge to authenticity? Page 19
- Read Philippians 4:11-13
- What did you learn from these verses?
- How would you describe the relationship between comparisons and contentment?
- Which is a bigger struggle for you authenticity or TMI?
- How can learning to apply Psalm 62:8 affect your relationships?
- Discuss responses to the question on page 21.
- Share updates about how each person is applying the reminders learned so far. Add any names to the collective list and celebrate any positive interactions that are taking pace. Take a few minutes for people to share any of the hindrances they're encountering and brainstorm some ideas to help them past those. Close by praying for the people on the list and for each group member to continue to persevere and be obedient.

Reminder Four

WATCH YOUR WORDS

- Find a few tweets or facebook posts that either really encourage you or really shock you. Don't identify who posted them but read each aloud and ask the group to share what they can deduce about the person who posted each just by hearing what was posted. Relate that to reminder 4 about the power of our words.
- Refer to page 22 and the verses listed. Ask members to share what they learned from one of the verses.
- Ask; Who are some people that God has allowed across your path that you uniquely related to? page 23
- Lead a discussion on the temptation to load people down with "you should" and what we learned about that concept? How have you seen or experienced the truth of this reminder?
- Ask: Have you ever experienced the language barrier of 'christianese'? Share any that come to mind.
- Discuss how some of the common church phrases can sound to a lost person? Page 24
- Add your own examples to the list of christianese phrases or terms.
- Ask members to share why they think we need to be careful about using these terms.
- Ask: What was Paul willing to do to reach people with the Gospel?
- Ask: How does that or should that affect you?
- Lead a discussion of what holds each person back from being like Paul.
- Take time to share ideas of how members can overcome the challenges they just shared.
- Refer to page 27 and encourage the group to share how it makes them feel to realize how many people have a skewed view of God and what they can do to help refute those wrong thoughts.
- Share updates and concerns about the relationships that members are developing. Add any names to the collective list and pray for the lost by name. Pray also for group members to be aware of what they are saying and to be more sensitive to how their words affect people.

Reminder Five

LET THE HOLY SPIRIT BE THE HOLY SPIRIT

- Share an example of a time when you tried to be the Holy Spirit for someone else. Stress that we have all had those moments when we have tried to be in control. Ask: How well does that usually go?
- Discuss the 'club mentality' concept that many churches have and what each of the group can do going forward to be more open to involving new people.
- Which of the better coaching practices spoke to you the most? Why?
- Refer to page 32 and talk about the value of sending people to Scripture for their answers. How does it benefit both the asker and the answerer?
- Lead a discussion of why it is important to not overreact. Page 33
- What are some possible consequences if you do overreact?
- As pointed out on page 34, discuss the value of people wrestling through things with the Lord for themselves.
- Ask: Have you ever tried to turn a new believer into a clone of you?
- Instead, who are we supposed to be becoming like according to 1 Corinthians 2:16?
- Lead a discussion of what each person needs to do differently in order to let go of control and trust in God's timing.
- Take a few minutes to share examples from Scripture that teach us what trying to manipulate circumstances can do instead of waiting on God's timing. (think Sarah & Abraham, David after his anointing, Joseph, etc) Point out that even when we don't understand why, we can trust that the Lord knows the big picture and the exact time things need to happen.
- Share updates on building relationships and add any new names to the collective prayer list. Pray specifically for people mentioned that are struggling this week. Invite the Holy Spirit to be present and to be in control. Pray for strength and wisdom and discernment for group members.

Reminder Six

ENJOY THE RIDE

- Spend the first few minutes of your time by listing all your favorite things about living for Christ and allowing Him to use you to reach other people with the Gospel.
- See page 37 and add some of your favorite things about doing life with new believers.
- Lead a discussion on why it is valuable to reflect on things you love about being used by God.
- Read through the story in Acts 8 together and challenge the group to point out parts of the story that illustrates each reminder and thing learned in this study. Use the questions in the book to guide your discussion as needed.
- What has been the most powerful aspect of this study to you? Why?
- Encourage members to use whatever means they prefer to set reminders for themselves of the "reminders" they have learned and been applying.
- Commit to holding each other accountable to living differently in light of what they have been intentional about these past few weeks.
- Close by praying over your list again and sharing the updates available on each relationship. Set up a plan to keep up with each other so you can encourage and rejoice with one another going forward.

Use the graph to fill in the names or descriptions of people that you come in contact with. Then tear this page out of the book and post it somewhere, tuck it in your Bible or take a picture of it and use as your screen saver. Do SOMETHING to keep it in front of you as a reminder to be praying for these names and to be intentional about speaking Jesus to them and building relationships with them.

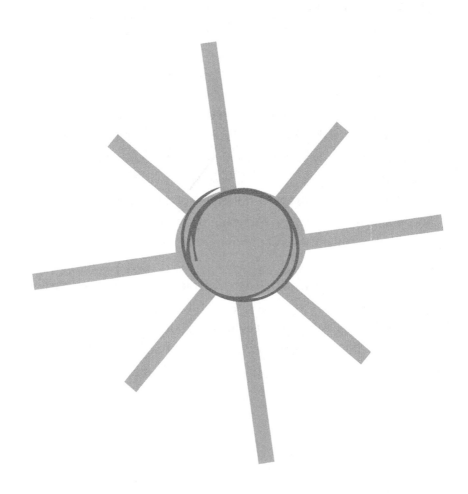

He said to them, "Go into all the world and preach the gospel to all creation".
Mark 16:15

Made in the USA
Coppell, TX
25 July 2020